STYLE ICONS

AUDREY HEPBURN

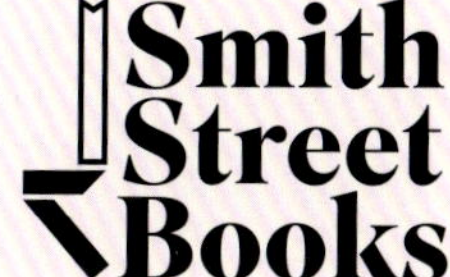

KELLY SMITH & ELIZABETH WEITZMAN

OUR FAIR LADY

AUDREY HEPBURN: STEEL CINDERELLA

Audrey Hepburn loved a fairytale. The film *Sabrina* literally begins with the words "Once upon a time …" and movie after movie finds her transformed from a sad single girl into a beloved sophisticate. Her early fans were often surprised to learn that their favorite screen princess was a serious and deeply intelligent woman who had faced immeasurable challenges in her youth. What's more, she drew on those experiences throughout her career, prioritizing children and charity over professional success.

Audrey Kathleen Hepburn-Ruston was born in Brussels, Belgium, on 4 May 1929. By the time she was six, her father had abandoned her to the care of her cold and exacting mother, the Baroness Ella van Heemstra. In 1939, they moved to the Netherlands in an attempt to avoid World War II, but the Germans invaded the country soon after. The impact of the Nazi occupation was immediate and acute, and they often survived on little more than water and nettles.

After the war, they moved to London, where Hepburn studied ballet and worked as a model to support the now-impoverished household. In 1951, at the age of twenty-two, Hepburn was discovered by the French writer Colette, who was so struck by her beauty that she impetuously cast the young unknown in the Broadway adaptation of her novel *Gigi.*

Hepburn's innate grace – a marked contrast to the hard-edged femme fatales of the 1940s and lush sex symbols of the 1950s – enraptured audiences immediately. In just fifteen years, she earned five Oscar nominations and came to personify style and sophistication.

Hepburn genuinely loved fashion, and encouraged others to see it as art. She found a sartorial soulmate in French designer Hubert de Givenchy and treasured their lifelong collaboration. By rejecting trends that didn't suit her, she taught her fans to trust their own instincts. And in staying true to herself, she redefined elegance itself.

And then … she gave it all up. In 1968, Hepburn went into semi-retirement in order to focus on her family. She loved being a mother, and believed her greatest purpose was to help children in need. Twenty years later, she became a full-time humanitarian. As an ambassador for UNICEF she visited orphanages, championed childhood immunizations, raised funds for clean water, and oversaw food distributions.

Sabrina may begin as a fairytale, but her character expresses Hepburn's own hard-won wisdom when she says, "I have learned how to be in the world and of the world, and not just to stand aside and watch."

Hepburn died at the age of 63 – far too young. However, decades after she captivated the world in films like *Roman Holiday* and *Breakfast at Tiffany's*, she remains as admired as ever. For as long as we continue to believe we can transform our lives through love (and an impeccable wardrobe), her impact will endure. And as for her elegance, glamour, and fashion legacy … that will always be *à la mode.*

INSTRUCTIONS

To use, carefully press out the doll and cross-piece and assemble the stand as shown below.

Use scissors to snip the cross-piece and stand.

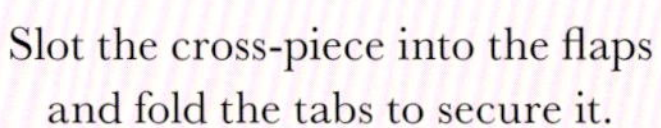

Slot the cross-piece into the flaps and fold the tabs to secure it.

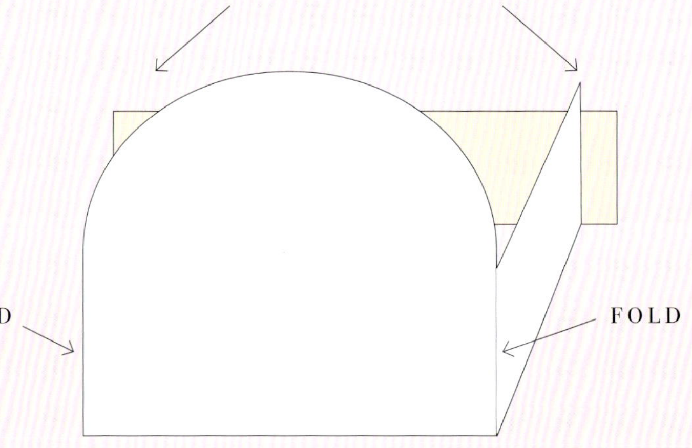

Press out the outfits and get dressing.
Style Audrey in her iconic looks, or mix and match
to create something brand new.

ROMAN HOLIDAY

DIRECTED BY WILLIAM WYLER

Believe it or not, Hepburn's big break almost didn't happen.

Roman Holiday is a sweet story about a runaway princess named Ann, who enlists an undercover reporter (played by Gregory Peck) for a thrilling day of freedom.

Inspired by the headline-generating romance between England's Princess Margaret and her commoner boyfriend, the role was originally meant for Hollywood royalty – Elizabeth Taylor. When director William Wyler decided he needed someone more regal, he offered it to elegant British star Jean Simmons. However, as Simmons was locked into a studio contract, Wyler reluctantly screen-tested five unknown actresses in the search for his princess.

Hepburn later said of her audition, "I was so green, I didn't really know what to do." But Wyler's recollections were far more positive. "Acting, looks, and personality! She was absolutely enchanting. We said, 'That's the girl!'"

She certainly was. Legendary costume designer Edith Head (who would win her fifth Oscar for this film) created this down-to-earth ensemble for Princess Ann's incognito adventures around Rome. At the beginning of the film, Audrey is dressed in a series of gorgeous, grandiose gowns as her character performs her royal duties across Europe, but it is this simple look that has endured, on and off the screen, after so many years. Head knew that this outfit, with its perfectly full skirt and belt, casually rolled button-down shirt, striped silk neck tie, and ankle-wrap sandals – as well as Ann's newly short, impossibly chic hairstyle – would allow the young star's regal poise to shine.

Hepburn's performance in her very first leading role didn't just launch her into instant stardom, it earned her an Academy Award for Best Actress.

1953

SABRINA

DIRECTED BY BILLY WILDER

With all eyes on her after the sweeping success of *Roman Holiday*, Hepburn knew she needed a truly worthy follow-up. She found it in Billy Wilder's romantic comedy, *Sabrina*. Hepburn plays an ordinary girl – a quiet chauffeur's daughter – who is wooed by wealthy brothers (Humphrey Bogart and William Holden). While Sabrina is first introduced to audiences in bare feet and a pinafore, she later returns from a trip to Paris as a new woman, with a wardrobe to match. Designed by no less than Hubert de Givenchy.

Hepburn's collaboration with Givenchy would last a lifetime, and *Sabrina* represents a literal and visible shift in her approach to fashion. Although Edith Head was the film's official designer, Hepburn visited Givenchy during the shoot to ask for his input. He gave her the run of his 1953 spring/summer collection, and she chose three outfits, all of which made it into the film.

Givenchy and Head never agreed on credits for this movie. Head won yet another Oscar, claiming that she had designed it all with some suggestions from him. Givenchy, meanwhile, argued that the film's most iconic outfits came straight from his atelier.

One of those dresses was this breathtaking organdy ball gown, embellished with an over-skirt train and jet-beaded embroidery. Complete with low-heeled classic black pumps and white gloves, Sabrina wears it to her first ball after she returns from Paris, newly determined to win true love.

Both the gown and Audrey worked their magic, of course.

1954

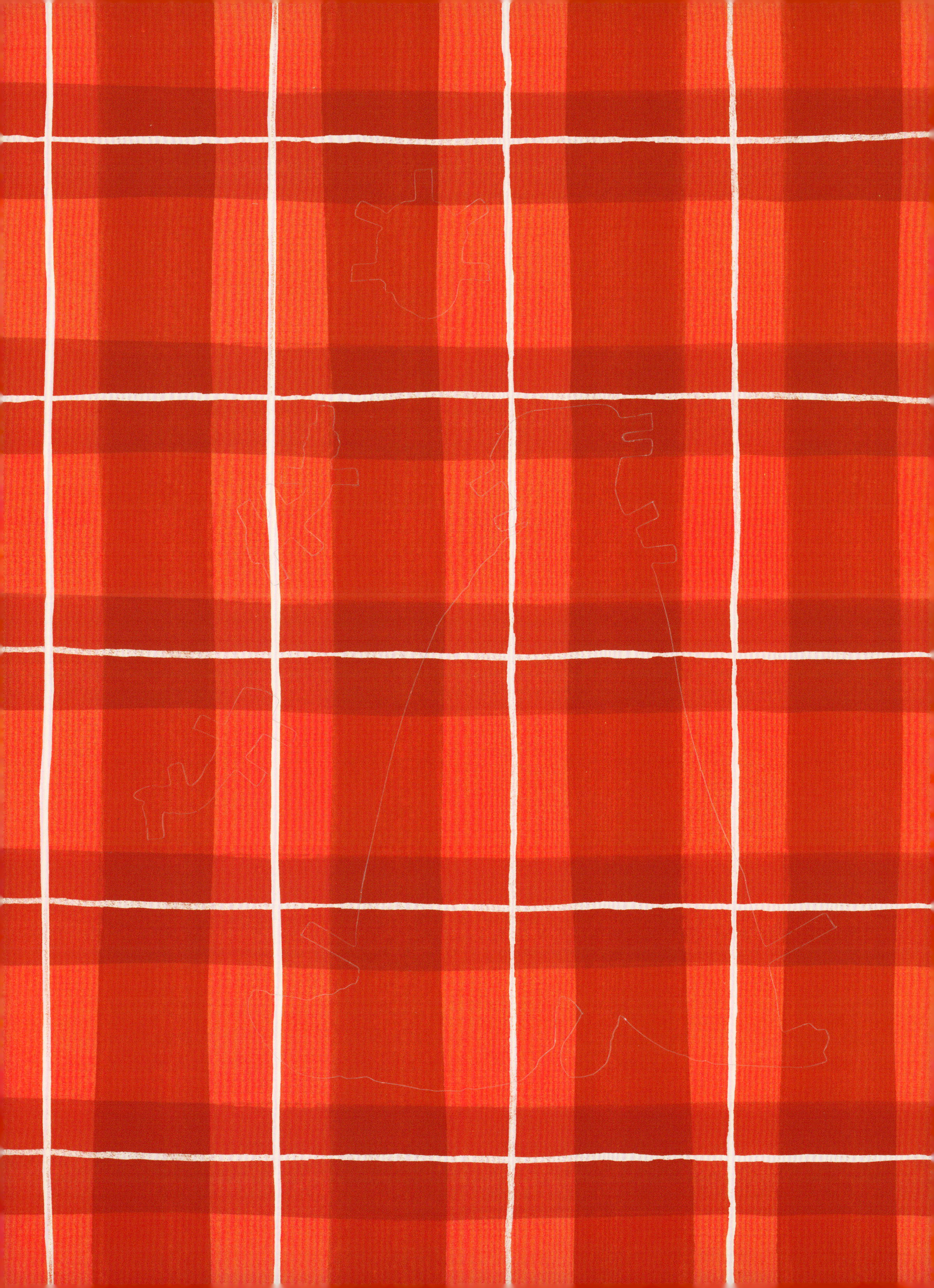

FUNNY FACE

DIRECTED BY STANLEY DONEN

After the tremendous response she received for her first few films, Hepburn now held the reins of her career. She wanted to make a Parisian musical with Fred Astaire and *Funny Face* – loosely inspired by a Broadway show Astaire made in 1927 – felt like the perfect fit.

In *Funny Face*, Hepburn again plays an independent young woman who is split between two styles: charmingly casual and stunningly chic.

As Greenwich Village intellectual, Jo, Hepburn wears black cigarette pants with a simple black sweater, a look that pulled the underground beatnik aesthetic into the mainstream. When Jo is discovered by a fashion editor (played by Kay Thompson, who – trivia alert – also wrote the *Eloise* books), she's swept off on a whirlwind trip to France.

And it's in Paris, amid models and *la mode*, that Jo discovers her love for the high fashion she once disdained. During a days-long shoot with a fashion photographer, Dick (Astaire), she dons a sequence of ever-more dazzling designs. When she emerges from behind the Louvre's famous Winged Victory statue wearing this strapless scarlet column gown with its train and matching chiffon stole, Dick is stunned. "Holy Moses!" he exclaims, on behalf of us all. "You look fabulous!" And rumour has it that those bedazzling emerald jewels were on special loan to Ms. Hepburn by Wallis Simpon, Duchess of Windsor.

Funny Face is given genuine depth by its leading lady – Hepburn was an undeniably thoughtful woman who treated fashion as a true art form. And, this time, she ensured that alongside "Costumes by Edith Head," the credits also read "Miss Hepburn's Paris Wardrobe by Hubert de Givenchy."

1957

➔ Place the stole behind the legs of the Audrey doll, then gently pull the gloves in front of her arms to attach.

LOVE IN THE AFTERNOON

DIRECTED BY BILLY WILDER

It's important to remember that in 1957, women's fashion was still trending towards high heels, flared skirts, and bullet bras. By the time Hepburn made *Love in the Afternoon*, she'd already had a significant influence on fashion – her ballet flats, capri pants, and clean lines were seen on sophisticates worldwide. But with *Love in the Afternoon*, her instinct for understatement found its most straightforward outlet.

Unlike her previous films, this is not a Cinderella story – although Wilder's offbeat romance does allow for some of Hepburn's trademark transformations. Her Ariane, a wide-eyed music student who secretly falls for a jaded playboy (played by Gary Cooper), briefly impersonates a mink-clad femme fatale in an attempt to impress him. But Ariane is most comfortable when she dresses more like herself, as represented by this youthful, low-key picnic outfit. In this scene, she wears elegant, striped capri pants with a white button-down and collared cardigan. The look is finished with playful accents of red, including a cummerbund, leather ballet flats and two sweet red bows atop Ariane's pigtails.

Even though the film wasn't a huge hit, Hepburn embraced the opportunity to reunite with Wilder and shoot another film in her beloved Paris. More importantly for fans, it gave them a whole new wardrobe to fall in love with and emulate.

1957

PARIS PURSUITS

PHOTOSHOOT

PHOTOGRAPHED BY RICHARD AVEDON

Hepburn's 1957 film *Funny Face* told the story of a young woman ushered into the world of haute couture by an imperious magazine editor and a visionary photographer – the former inspired by real-life *Harper's Bazaar* editor Diana Vreeland, and the latter based on the renowned fashion photographer Richard Avedon.

Fantasy met reality when Vreeland's *Harper's Bazaar* featured Hepburn in a fashion editorial titled "Paris Pursuits," shot by none other than Avedon. "Paris Pursuits" starred Hepburn as "Jemima Jones, a traveling actress" alongside comedy actors Zsa Zsa Gabor, Buster Keaton and Hepburn's husband Mel Ferrer.

In this feature, Vreeland was cementing the status of not one, but two fashion icons. Fabled French designer Christian Dior had died just two years earlier, leaving his fashion empire to his twenty-one-year-old protégé, Yves Saint Laurent. In having the already-revered Hepburn showcase Saint Laurent's exquisite designs – including this tulle Armide cocktail dress, described in the magazine as a "white crystallized puffed tunic silhouette" – Vreeland was anointing Saint Laurent as Dior's worthy successor. The shimmering fairytale of a dress was elevated by a memorable coiffure by Enrico Caruso, white strappy heels and opera gloves, and extravagant jewels.

1959

BREAKFAST AT TIFFANY'S: OPENING SCENE

DIRECTED BY BLAKE EDWARDS

Well, this is it, isn't it? It's the poster that's graced a million bedroom walls. The scene that's inspired countless newcomers to New York. The look that transformed Hepburn from contemporary icon into timeless legend.

And once again, it almost didn't happen.

Truman Capote, who wrote the novella on which *Breakfast at Tiffany's* is based, insisted that only one woman could portray his heroine Holly Golightly: Marilyn Monroe. Hepburn was, of course, the opposite of Monroe in many ways. What's more, she agreed with Capote. A melancholy tale of a desperate Southern call girl barely hanging on in the big city? That wasn't her.

But the film's producers wanted Hepburn, and her husband and unofficial manager, the actor Mel Ferrer, urged her to reconsider. After some necessary adjustments to the script, Hepburn's subtler version of Holly found its pathos in the contrast between her continental charm, defiant bravado, and hidden vulnerability. The beautifully modulated performance earned her another Oscar nomination.

But let's be honest, it's this opening scene that we all remember best. Givenchy's coveted "little black dress." At first appearing devastatingly simple this black gown was in fact meticulously tailored and filled with horsehair stuffing and lead weights to perfect its drape down to the very last detail. It becomes an elegant satin canvas for Holly's Oliver Goldsmith sunglasses, glistening Swarovski tiara and earrings, strands upon strands of Roger Scemama–designed pearls, satin elbow-length gloves, kitten heels, and *that* cigarette holder. Givenchy's oh-so-sleek gown, with its ultra-extra accoutrements, reveals Holly's true identity perfectly. She is an unapologetic striver who knows she can only afford to *look* at Tiffany's shimmer – and makes a meal of it anyway.

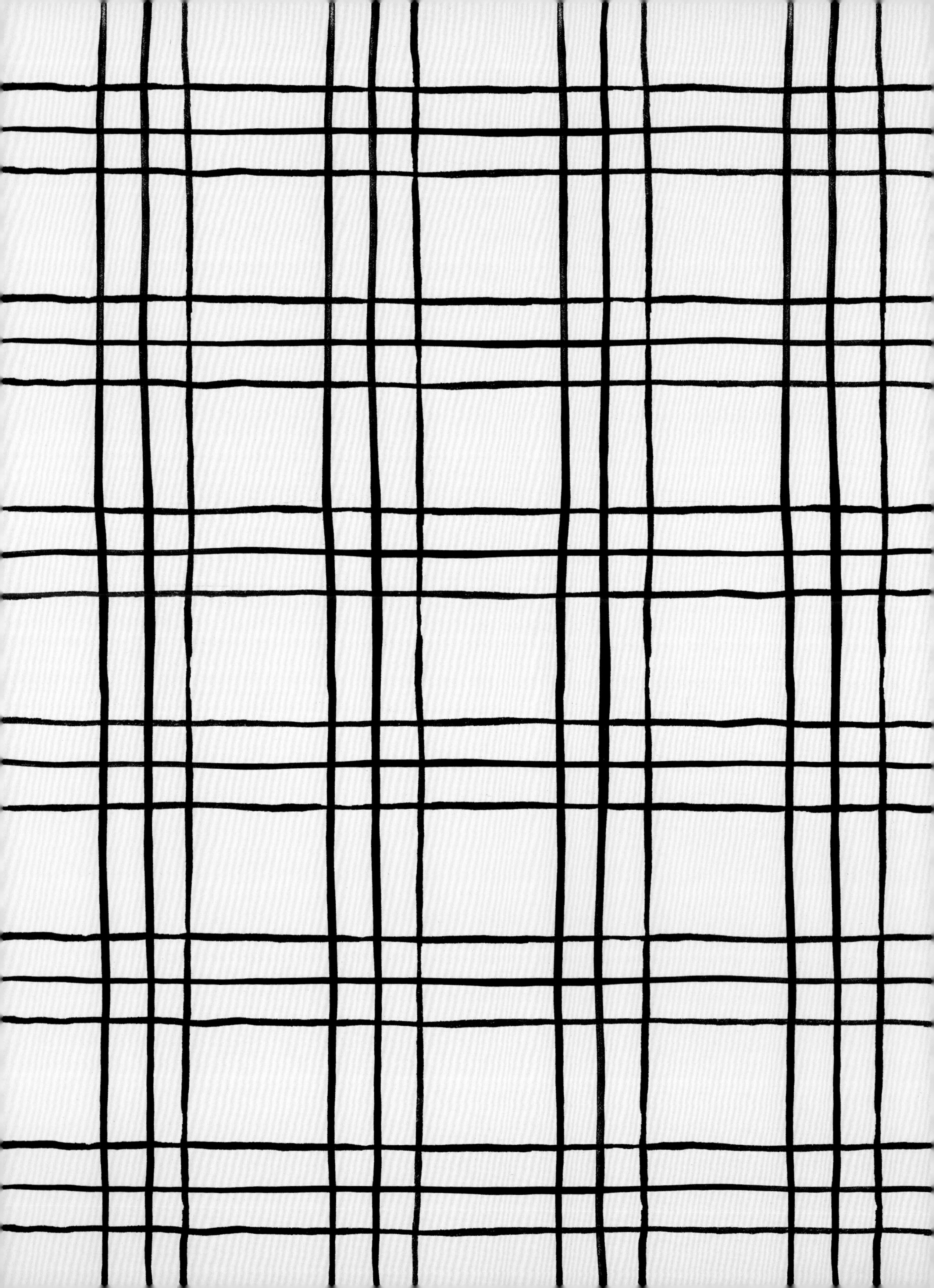

1961

BREAKFAST AT TIFFANY'S: HOLLY MEETS PAUL

DIRECTED BY BLAKE EDWARDS

The sheer glamour of *Breakfast at Tiffany's* – the Givenchy dresses, the glittering jewels, Hepburn's luminous beauty – is enough to keep it famous forever. But let's not forget that Hepburn was far more than a natural clotheshorse. She was a gifted performer whose empathetic portrayal of Holly's inner life continues to elevate this film decades after it was made.

It was essential to Hepburn that her portrayal of Holly Golightly represented every young woman who arrives in a big city with outsized dreams, only to find herself facing a far grittier reality.

In one scene, Holly's neighbor, Paul, wakes her after she's collapsed into bed, with her loving Cat by her side, at the end of a very late night. She has clearly been nude beneath her sheets, with the exception of her aspirational Tiffany blue sleep mask and lavender tasseled earrings. The inference is that the oversized tuxedo shirt she has just grabbed off the floor belongs to a boyfriend ... or perhaps even (it's ever so slightly suggested) a *client*. We're meant to understand, in other words, that Holly is no virgin – a rather shocking implication in 1961.

We see Holly's innocence challenged again when she indulges in some coy shoplifting at a five-and-dime store, in order to "keep her hand in," as she explains to Paul. The pair steal plastic cat and dog masks, and Holly uses hers to accessorize her gorgeous orange Givenchy double-breasted coat, before brazenly walking out the front door onto the street. While her morals may be in doubt, her style certainly is not.

1961

PARIS WHEN IT SIZZLES

DIRECTED BY RICHARD QUINE

Hepburn was nothing if not loyal, and this postmodern romp finds her back in France with *Breakfast at Tiffany's* screenwriter George Axelrod and her *Sabrina* costar – and longtime friend – William Holden.

As Gabrielle, a secretary hired by Richard, Holden's American playboy screenwriter, she arrives for duty carrying her birdcage. If you look closely, you can see the yellow cover says "Richelieu," because the bird is – get it? – a cardinal. (And if you don't get it, don't worry. Cardinal Richelieu was a famous French priest and politician in the seventeenth century.)

Despite this little quirk, Gabrielle's crisp pale green wool skirt suit, short-brimmed straw hat, and smart kitten heels (Givenchy again, of course) reflect her no-nonsense approach and foreshadow the dramatic contrast between the pair. He's such a mess that she has to repeatedly rescue him from his own procrastination.

Eventually they write the screenplay together, conjuring a series of fantasy scenarios that see Hepburn playing everything from a pilot to a spy. In between, director Richard Quine packs the film with amusing industry jokes, and cameos from the likes of Tony Curtis, Marlene Dietrich, and even Hepburn's husband, Mel Ferrer.

Fun fact: This is believed to be the first time a designer ever received onscreen credit for perfume, thanks to the signature scent (L'Interdit) Givenchy created for his magnificent muse.

PARIS WHEN IT SIZZLES

1964

MY FAIR LADY

DIRECTED BY GEORGE CUKOR

With *My Fair Lady*, Hepburn embodied another version of the Cinderella story, this time as Cockney flower seller Eliza Doolittle. Again, her casting was quite controversial. Julie Andrews and Rex Harrison – playing Eliza's tutor – had originated the lead roles in Lerner and Loewe's enormously popular Broadway production, based on George Bernard Shaw's *Pygmalion*. When Harrison was hired for the film, but Andrews wasn't, theatergoers were outraged. And it definitely didn't help when word leaked that most of Hepburn's singing had been dubbed – against her wishes – by Marni Nixon.

Nevertheless, *My Fair Lady* was embraced by audiences and became the second-highest grossing film of 1964. It also won Best Picture, Best Director for George Cukor, and Best Actor for Harrison (who diplomatically dedicated his Oscar to his "*two* fair ladies"). Andrews did receive her own flowers that night, winning Best Actress for her role in *Mary Poppins* – which also happened to become the year's top moneymaker.

For *My Fair Lady*, costume designer Cecil Beaton created a remarkable 1,500 outfits, but none more gorgeous than this gown that Eliza wears to the stunningly stylized Royal Ascot race. The scene, imagined almost entirely in shades of black and white, marks Eliza's tentative entry into society. She hasn't quite got it right yet – witness the crowd's shock when she exhorts her horse to "move yer bloomin' arse!" – but she certainly enchanted viewers.

The lace confection she is wearing – a black and white mermaid-style gown and show-stopping matching hat and parasol – was inspired by Beaton's own memories of an elite Edwardian childhood. In 2011, it was sold at auction for US$3.7 million.

1964

TWO FOR THE ROAD

DIRECTED BY STANLEY DONEN

As she neared the end of this stage of her acting career – before taking a break to focus on family – Hepburn felt ready to expand her persona. And, of course, her wardrobe.

Two for the Road took her away from couture into a more modern, ready-to-wear style. Hepburn and director Stanley Donen shopped off the rack to get the edgier look they wanted. As a result, the credits read "Miss Hepburn's clothes by Ken Scott, Michèle Rosier, Paco Rabanne, Mary Quant, Foale and Tuffin, and others."

The film's plot is strikingly sharp. Hepburn and Albert Finney play Joanna and Mark, a miserable, middle-aged married couple (which, at the time, meant they were in their mid-thirties). They spend most of the movie recalling the many road trips that have shaped – and strained – their relationship.

Interestingly, the characters' wardrobes shift along with their emotions. Both are portrayed as being happiest in their penniless early days, when they're wearing jeans and sneakers. The posher their lives and outfits become, the more disconnected they are.

This fab Miss Dior knitted boyshort bikini, white YUHU Oliver Goldsmith sunglasses, and the vinyl Michèle Rosier cover-up (overleaf) are expensive upgrades from the simple one-piece Joanna donned during an early date with Mark. Instead of sunbathing happily with her love on an isolated stretch of sand, she wears it at a crowded beach club as the barely speaking duo sulkily order lobster from their lounge chairs.

Don't fret, though, Hepburn would never allow things to go *too* far off track. As her character insists to the finish, "I love happy endings."

1967

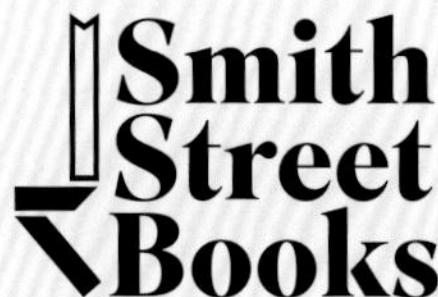

Published in 2026 by Smith Street Books
Naarm (Melbourne) | Australia
smithstreetbooks.com

Distributed outside of ANZ, North & Latin America by
Thames & Hudson Ltd., 6–24 Britannia Street, London, WC1X 9JD
thamesandhudson.com

EU Authorised Representative: Interart S.A.R.L.
19 rue Charles Auray, 93500 Pantin, Paris, France
productsafety@thameshudson.co.uk; www.interart.fr

ISBN: 978-1-9232-3980-7

Smith Street Books respectfully acknowledges the Wurundjeri People of the Kulin Nation, who are the Traditional Owners of the land on which we work, and we pay our respects to their Elders past and present.

Publisher: Hannah Koelmeyer
Project editor: Lucy Grant
Illustrator: Kelly Smith
Design & layout: Susan Le
Text: Elizabeth Weitzman
Text editor: Lorna Hendry
Proofreader: Cressida McDermott
Prepress: Megan Ellis
Production manager: Aisling Coughlan

Printed & bound in China by C&C Offset Printing Co., Ltd.

Unofficial and unauthorized. This title is not affiliated in any way with Audrey Hepburn's estate and/or heirs.

Book 437
10 9 8 7 6 5 4 3 2 1